MEDITATION OF THE DAMNED

Written by
ONEIKE BARNETT

Edited by Derville Lowe

Copyright © 2021 Oneike Barnett.
All rights reserved.

No part of this book may be used or reproduced by any means, whether electronically or physically (photocopying, photographing, etc.) or stored on any medium for use or retreival, except in the case of purchased eBooks and brief excerpts for articles and reviews, without written permission from the author.

Due to the dynamic nature of the Internet, any links or web addresses shared in this book may have been changed or updated after the publication of this book and may no longer be valid.

This book contains mature themes and situations and uses strong language. It is not for use by children. The content may be sensitive for some readers. Reader discretion is strongly advised.

Any photographs, illustrations, imagery or depiction of people used herein are provided by the author for illustrative purposes only and are not of real people, unless otherwise noted. All photos are used by permission.

Original Cover Art by Oneike Barnett
Cover & Interior Design by Norwood Creative Hub
norwoodcreativehub.godaddysites.com

Books by this author are available on Amazon, through booksellers or by contacting:

Oneike Barnett
Montego Bay, Jamaica
barnettsfarm357@gmail.com

Contents

Biological Time Bomb 1

Black and Proud 3

Bon Appetit 5

Change the Narrative 6

Death 8

Elusive 9

Endurance 11

Envy 13

Gun Perspective 15

Hours 17

Hypocrisy 19

It 20

Karma 21

Late Night Groove 23

Money 24

Mother 26

New World Order 28

One Don 30

Reality Check 32

Sheeples	34
Stranded	35
Thankful	37
The Love of Hate	39
Behind the Eyelids	41
Cold Truth	43
Fluidity	45
Ghetto Mentality	47
Humility Rules	49
Lascivious	51
Way Up	53
Pretense	55
Pandemic	57

MEDITATION OF THE DAMNED

Biological Time Bomb

Look at your watches, face time, let your thoughts inspire awe and admiration, sublime. The destructive messages conveyed to us by society is below the threshold of our consciousness, subliminal, disrupt what is perceived to be the norm and you are labelled a criminal.

For the simple fact that you the prey outwitted the Fox you're chastised for thinking outside of the box, everything they do is right, until a civilian tries it, once their profits ignite in court you have an arsonist, larceny charge to fight.

What the eyes don't see the heart don't leap, I suddenly realised that ninety-nine point nine percent of the people on Earth are asleep, all weary from the seducers tricks unaware we're caught in the Matrix. Intoxicated on euphoria is God going to destroy this new Sodom and Gomorrah?

How are the students supposed to learn if the pundits don't practice what they teach? Is it not nonsense? Use your conscience, because common sense isn't so common at all; we see evil's steady rise, while good constantly falls.

Don't sell your spiritual warmth to get to the next level, the ruler of this Twenty-First Century is the devil and his minions, take a good look around, you're all entitled to your own opinions. They know what they're doing and they do it well, this is not heaven.

Starvation, sufferation, wars, decay and death, empty shells of our former selves is the only thing that's left. Mimicking all we see, gesturing without words as if we are all mimes, what will it be called when all the biological watches on Earth self-destruct? END TIMES.

Black and Proud

Damaging our hair with chemicals, bleaching ruining our skin; replicating Caucasians, trying to blend in. Believing black is wrong and white is right. Brainwashed. Constantly bombarded with white superiority propaganda feeling inferior despising our God-given exterior.

Convinced we have committed some unforgivable sin cause of the colour of our skin. Condemning ourselves to failure even though we are designed to win.

Self-decay artificially implanted in our psyche not our DNA, yet we self-destruct day by day. Cruising in simulation mode docility is the code, passive, too ignorant to see this is high-tech Slavery.

Then their biggest labour force, now their biggest consumers spending more than the majority and we are the poorest minority. Bewitched, trapped in a trance, the puppeteers pull the strings and we, their puppets, dance.

We've been enduring for years, blood, sweat and tears, lets relinquish self-hate and start loving ourselves and our peers, black is beautiful.

Let's take control of our minds, our assets; unite, help each other gain the courage to fight against the subliminal black inferiority, white superiority messages.

Emancipating, educating, creating, circulating positive messages of black power that are innating, demonstrating that we are the embodiment of infinite possibilities. Let's stop settling for the sequel, we are all created equal.

Bon Appétit

Females are beautiful, cursed meals; waiting for someone to gobble them up. A bottomless cup that can't be filled, in your pursuit you're emotionally killed.

Drained of your soul, your existence, now an empty shell assuming it's well. Sustained by Eve's apple yet committed no sin.

Though condemned to your conscience, don't judge your experience it teaches, wise or dumb, the choice lingers.

Squeal after your meal, rapid heartbeat, a taste that's bitter-sweet; sweaty palms, fidgeting feet, pleasurable indigestion. Bon Appétit.

Change the Narrative

I spent my childhood in a wild hood, not law abiding as they thought I should. Good but I could if the circumstances were different. I probably would be on honor roles instead of a collector of souls, or among the upper echelons instead of with those who wish they weren't born to suffer; where survival meant you have to be rougher and tougher.

Here your neighbors have nothing, so they are willing to take your nothingness if you let them and vice versa. Putting you in a hearse to quench their hunger and thirst, then say it's the white man's curse why we're worst than we ever been; when we normalize what is considered to be sin and create the nightmares we live in.

The wild hood like the wild, wild west, shots rang off - Bang! Bang! No vest, two in the head, four in the chest, now you're lying on the ground from a normal sound. Deceased, six shots, six foot six, dead bodies are the least, they're everywhere.

How can there be peace when there's no respect or care for your peer? What is fear when guns are here with bullets to spare? Steeple housing, our names ring bells, clout chasers, empty shells. Hiding behind masks to make wishes come through; wishing well, flipping coins, buying the illusions they sell.

But there's no refund for dead sons, all we do is protest guns and start losing daughters. What's the next generation without mothers or fathers? Extinct. This is how we're programmed to think, drag each other down so we all can sink; no elevation. Then what is to profit?

Is self interest human or you one? Come on let's stop it, quit, put a cap on the bull shit. Seek knowledge, absorb it so you can speak the truth so the seeds you sow know its roots, shoot and bear positive, digestible fruits.

Death

To all that is living it's certain. You can run, hide away or will it to come another day? Where it takes you, nobody knows; just a solitary experience with your eyelids closed.

Some say it's the cousin of sleep, its abysmal ache causes our love ones to weep. Whether it was wasted or a life well spent, all is left is just memories, eternal lament; until we ourselves expire, our physical remnants buried or destroyed by fire.

It burrows through your skin, flesh, bones take control, seizing your soul. From the inception of time its cyclical finesse never grows old; with life it's an alliance, its reign eluding science, crippling from the minuscule upwards to the giants.

At the snap of a finger, it leaves you paralyzed forever; numb, it creates an equilibrium. So, wipe the tears from your eyes, stop asking "why?" and accept this fact - all that is alive, must die.

Elusive

Accepting constant change, only change is constant, spending big bills, popping pills to get closer to reality. She's elusive, the woman of my dreams, nothing is as it seems.

Sometimes less is more, yet my addiction is overdosing on this whore called fiction, trying to acquire it all ignoring my limit that's greed. When your wants are more important than your basic needs.

You're derailed if your needs aren't met, yet you still want, you've failed. The one who needs you the most is looking in the mirror, I'm not a hero.

For heroically saving me from a burning building and the world winding like a tornado, this incessant spiralling out of control, gaining control, trying to save my soul from eternal damnation, salvaging salvation.

Only to repeat – "am I sane?" In my mind I'm fine, eating grapes, sipping wine, I unwind. While being evaluated by society - my psychiatrist, who says I'm iconic; how ironic this life is - you can relate.

Like Wikipedia our information accessible on social media, public records following the famous, in the process we lose us.

Oxy-numb, broken pieces, scraped together thinking; problem solved with technological strains, we insanely evolved into machines, instruments, programmable beings. Programmed to self-destruct from behind the scenes by enlightened beings.

Alive with vacant heads, dead before we died; we haven't lived, this isn't life. Soul searching, with our souls churched in; dogma in one hand, in the other is conceptual sin. Can we win?

The finish line keeps moving, our worthiness needs proving; nothing is without impunity, living like I have immunity. Sprinting bare feet is actuality, still can't grasp reality. Hamsters on a wheel, twirl and twirl; what's the use of being sane in an insane world?

Endurance

Have you ever been hurt so bad that your pain feels pain, your numb feels numb, your only question is "how come"? When your broken heart breaks and the shattered pieces shatter; imagine standing in lava, only ten times hotter.

Even with all this suffering some how you survived, yet you're pondering if you should be thankful or upset that you're still alive. When it's like being paralyzed and you can only move your eyes, they keep perching on your nose and you can't even fan the flies.

So, you start questioning everything because your doubt has doubts, wondering if it's ever going to rain because your drought has droughts.

Can't empathize with yourself when your sorry feels sorry and the burden that you're carrying has a burden that it carries. Putting yourself in a predicament, where your confuse is confused and you have no one to blame because you had the choice to choose.

Meditation of the Damned   *Oneike Barnett*

Now your snot drains snot and your tears cry tears, you're afraid to be afraid because your fears got fears. You continue to daydream but you're living nightmares, with no resolution, no help from your peers.

This dilemma occurs day after day, you pray for it to stop, but it keeps on happening anyway. Then you suddenly realize you're alone, secluded without a friend; so your hope hangs on to hope that one day this shit will end.

Envy

People aren't shit, but flush them anyway. Venomous snakes, can't touch them anyway. Pay attention to what they do, never listen to what they say; no solid foundation, relations, built on top of clay.

Seeing you with something new automatically his is old, blood vessel pops in his eyes as his heart turns cold. Imagining death for you, as if taking yours is the only way he'll ever win; ready to repeat Cain's sin, it matters not if you're his kin.

African, Caucasian, etc. humans, brothers, though from another mother, it's our thought process that makes one different from the other. His deceitful thoughts - "You know, I'm really happy for you, had you in my prayers praying your dreams would come true; my brother, just keep up the good work, you're the true definition of work, you work to make things work."

His true thoughts, no pretence - "Stay lucky you little jerk, my time is now, on you I'm about to put in work. Take your shit, Bang! Bang! Buss your head split. Go ball, buy fancy stuff in the mall, you

gave me a little but I wanted it all." Oh my, with
teary eyes amidst sobs and cries at your funeral,
he's faking goodbyes. Fuck it, maggots and flies
release your soul, he's Eskimo cold; now you're a
victim.

Do you really want to be a victim? Evict him.
Change him like your phone sim and re-up, hurry
up and move on. Don't pet a poisonous snake,
your mistake will be like an earthquake, with
sinkhole that swallows you whole digested.

Change the narrative the way you live, of course
you must forgive; but use a sieve and surround
yourself with all that's positive.

Gun Perspective

Why am I used, abused, then blamed for your actions? You are the intelligent, empathic ones - Humans!

I, on the other hand is an inanimate object, comprised of mechanical parts, built for one purpose and one purpose only, to kill, something I can never do without you. Your will, your choice, your decision; life and death are in your hands.

I am Gun, I can't refuse to be used. Your wish is my very command. My babies stop your babies from living, my giving stops your living from giving.

I can't sin, so I have no need to repent. On me a lot of time, energy and money is spent, so that I in return, can take away your time, energy and let others spend money to you bury.

I don't love or care for no one, I'm loyal to no one, respect no one. Even though I belong to you, if you point me to your head with one in my chamber and squeeze my trigger, your dead.

I can't be charged, prosecuted or executed; to me your laws aren't applicable. If you're looking for the real culprits responsible for the heinous crimes of which I'm being accused, look in the mirror.

Hours

You would think I'm time to how they watch, saying I'm at it again but they don't want me to gain so they're on their knees praying for me to fall like rain; but I'm the cloud, not thunder, silently flashing like lightening but to them I'm loud. Ladies love me well endowed, no bleacher, I'm black and proud.

Yes, black lives matter but my gun won't discriminate when making spleen disintegrate and innards splatter; lacerated liver taking enemies lives as if I was the giver, yet I fathered none.

I have guns that are nuns yet eager to fuck like prostitutes. Dunce niggers just waiting for me to say shoot, so they can uproot your soul like weeds. On souls they feed, literally smoking people like weed, getting high from deducting what you need, your life.

Envy is dangerous, jealousy is forbidden; observe those you keep close because behind a smile both are hidden.

Watch your table, always remember Cain and Abel, so even your own blood could be covetously unstable.

Still, I live asking God to forgive those who trespass against me, not knowing what they do or what I will do. As I do the do hustle, stay winning, getting through, helping all who stay true, so we all cross the finish line.

Being a champion is a hobby of mine. Refined, I fine dine, no rum, just red wine. Protecting my peace of mind, casting no pearls to no swine. Living, loving my wife, her name is life; for her I'm thankful.

Hypocrisy

What was your shared sentiments in that debate? It takes two to conversate. What was your demeanour? Were you irate, excited or disgusted? Hearing my name being lambasted by someone I trusted.

Did you show him the door or did you applause and request an encore? Don't say no more, just quit. Weren't you also talking shit, you hypocrite?

That's hypocrisy, slandering my name with him and his with me, that's exactly what you be. Can't you see? You're a propaganda machine propagating hate, pretending loyalty is your best trait, when unwanted turmoil is what you create.

Verbally deceiving, sealing your fate in hypocrisy. Scum, your dual information causes inflammation like gingivitis to the gum; from today forth you're not welcome.

Together we will no longer share a meal or sit. You don't like me, save your spit, stop the false pretence, you hypocrite.

It wants everything for itself, selfish indulgence, hoarding all to its side, a want not a need. Always over consuming, constantly feed, but it's never willing to share. When you hear its name, you quiver in fear; even if you have nothing, it will still take it from you without care.

To it, being obese is the least, all it thinks of is nourishment, a never-ending feast. Only words, savoury and palatable brings a smile to its face, acquire and gain, possessively insane. One who stops at nothing to receive and to obtain.

Its insatiable appetite cannot be appeased, all that is within sight best believe, will be seized. Its ravenous desires set it on a path to rob, pillage and plunder. If you're in its way you will pay for your blunder.

Gluttonous, avaricious - some of the names it is called. It despises charity bitterly, when they meet, they are both appalled. It is ever up and ready to reap, although it didn't plant a seed. This voracious "It" I speak of, do you know it? Its real name is *Greed*.

Karma

Standing with your back to the sun with an epiphany is no fun when the rabbit has the gun and there is no place to run. Looking left and right but help is nowhere in sight, now there is a lot on your mind, so you're mindful, that your antagonist has his hands full, pointing a gun with his finger on the trigger. Is it loaded?

Lord please don't let him pull, wishing you had a Red Bull that could actually give you wings. In your brain are random thoughts of staying alive, knowing your about to be dead from bullet holes, you're nostalgic. Was it something you said or did? Were you grown or a kid?

With your atrocious past, God forbid you can't remember. Was it December? Maybe January or February, contrary, the true reason occurred in rabbit season. Confused, you ask, "What have I done to deserve this?" Your face got an instant twist from freezing steal, you know it's real.

Gratitude is a burden, revenge is pleasurable to the soul; wishing you could apologize, you see dead in his eyes, they're stone cold. You trickle a little pee on yourself again from the physical and mental pain.

Your knees buckle as your palms get wet, drenched in cold sweat; palpitating heart, short of breath, wondering if there is life after death, it beckons. Everything occurring in under 60 seconds.

Now overwhelmed by remorseful thoughts of you being violent. Bang!!! Bang!!! Then it all goes silent.

Late Night Groove

Grooving, moving, rhythm improving, soothing to the soul so let go and let the beat take control. Dancing, the vibe is right, it's midnight. Non-stop 'til daylight, cruise, Jazz, Rhythm and Blues.

Grooving so mellow, the bass guitar, no cello, sets the mood. Puff-puff, sip-sip, on the most expensive brew, the dude with the highest grade, still not passing, my thoughts in a haze condones my selfish ways.

Bibidi-beep-bop, I won't stop, even when the beat stops, I'm on top of a cloud with an angel. She's dressed in white, her dress is tight, accentuating her curves, stimulating my nerves.

Whispered in her ear what she wants to hear, convinced now we're a pair, yes, a couple, so in the restroom we copulate. My pianist had her hitting high notes. Wax on, wax off, two coats, it's that good; so she savored it screaming I'm her favorite hit. Saturated by my sax, she climaxed.

Grooving, moving, rhythm improving, soothing to the soul, so let go and let the beat take control.

Money

One is the loneliest number, but zero has nothing. From nothing to something is spectaculous, hard work isn't miraculous. In God I trust, everyone else pays cash; taking no checks. If everything isn't good...I bounce.

Meddle with my livelihood and you'll pronounce, as sure as a pound is sixteen ounce. Warren Buffet of poetry chasing Warren Buffet for real, with wounds that won't heal, afflicted.

Pain either makes you strong or foolish, it's with strength that I do this. Turn pain into gain, constantly accumulating, while fools make it rain.

Seeking Bill Gates' glory, took pages from his book so I could live his story. Blueprint, patience is the foundation, no mad sprint. Building from the ground up, turn my frown from upside down, up.

Up is the charted course, lost nothing in my previous divorce from poverty, now engaged to wealth. Social status changed from a "have-not", now affiliated with the "haves" and the "have lots".

Butlers open doors to new spots acquired - apartments, hotels; standing in the lobby, residual income is my new hobby.

Real estate is my frame of mind, so I invest. Investment is now a game of mine, playing like its chess. Thinking further ahead, doing my best to be the best. Seeing what I believe, aiming to achieve heights of greatness; not attained by sudden flight, so I won't rest.

Insomnia, paranoia...breathtaking. Money is my love, nonstop love making. Intimate with big bills yet still fornicating with dime pieces. When wealth increases all else ceases to exist. Quick to use my fist as I'm quick to take risks, won't think twice seeking paradise.

That's too strange, when silver is behind transparency you do change. Without a sign, ain't searching for my mind, they said I've lost it, but I've tossed it, to survive in this crazy world, soul held hostage by a crazy girl, who can't feel. The illusion held together by billions convinced it's real.

To collect, I have to pay; can't leave I have to stay. Can't walk away, my overly ambitious egotistical self won't let me turn my back on this inanimate object that can't love, has no love that I love, it has no heart. So, I decommissioned my heart and took the solemn vow "'til death do us part".

#

Often taken for granted yet so integral, life's vertebral column, wholesome. For nine months you are a loner, at times neglected by the donor.

Unyielding, your indomitable maternal instinct kicks in, so you nurture and care for the young life you bring with laser-like precision. God's gift, not only to man, but to the world.

Mother, the distinguished title bestowed upon you, all that it personifies is true, only you are capable of the things you do.

A Goddess, a Queen, you deserve a throne; your young's survival rivals your own. Though mankind is unkind, your selfless love is divine, providing a piece of mind – no, a whole mind; your lessons impart a gold mind.

Those who doubt your importance are too blind to see that without you they wouldn't be in existence. Your strength, poise and consistence are no coincidence, you are resilient.

Even when your chances are slim and the future looks dim or pale, you refuse to fail.

Sustaining, maintaining, never complaining, possessing the will, you create a way toiling effectively day after day.

Woman, mother - compared to you there's no other. Love, honor, respect - to you is infinitely due.

All the mothers of the world - I solute you.

New World Order

Days turn to months, months into years, nothing is new under the sun. There is no positive change but no one even cares. Seconds turn to minutes, minutes into hours, this world is filled with abominable things as a result of man's obsession with power.

We disrupt nature, shifting the balance. As a race how can we grow? Convinced we have all the answers when we don't even know that we don't know not even half of the story, reaping the glory for something we ourselves can't be. Constantly staring at our reflections so ourselves is all we see.

Everything sells for a piece of paper, can't afford water, you're stuck with vapour; throat parched because you're dying of thirst. Starvation dehydration - which is worse?

Racial inequality. Aren't we all human beings? The word freedom is just food for thought, we are controlled by every means. Money, drugs, telecommunication, religion, food and weapons are some of the tools, oil is the fuel that the few uses to rule.

Wars fought in the name of profit, hoarding every penny. Love of lives they despise, their enterprise is to monopolize all they see with their eyes. Just so they can make a show, acting like they know what heaven is, playing God.

The name Lucifer now rings a bell because instead they have created hell, unveiling his biggest trick to the world. Convinced he didn't exist, now he rules with an iron fist; call me a conspiracy theorist but it's true.

The question is - what can you do when you're being manipulated too? Thinking you yourself is aware, when you really have no clue.

One Don

Him beloved like the hymn in the hymnal, yet labelled a criminal. For wanting to protect all like a superhero, the one you call to reinforce your wall and break your fall.

Envied by many who still don a smile, just to gain a penny or a shot of henny. Him like the hymn in the hymnal yet labelled a criminal, has an understanding cause where he's standing defers from where you sit.

Community flies don't tell lies beloved, cause he's the shit; respected, resilient, he'll never quit. To resolve ten thousand calls he never stalls.

Champion of his surroundings, heavy weight; Trismegistus, three times great. In him the community has faith to make things great again.

Him like the hymn in the hymnal, yet labelled a criminal; honorable, yet despised as a rebel. They could confine him for months saying he's an intellectual dunce for being unorthodox, for stepping out of the box.

Enlightening the flocks of political fallacies, misguided policies and procedures; this gave them seizers, convulsions, exacerbated by the thought of him being the man.

Him, like the hymn in the hymnal yet labelled a criminal; still loved by all who wants to see him stand tall.

Reality Check

I need residual earnings like the Harry Potter books they make, so like an oven I'm trying to bake this consistent cake, so when I step, I quake the Earth. Though this isn't all life is worth, it isn't cheap, so I keep mining to ensure my pockets are deep.

Steadily hoarding this trash called cash, wanting piles of garbage that feeds me to buy all you see, since nothing including freedom isn't free, I got to secure my entry fee.

This keeps me searching for traction, that thing that no matter how much you have, there is no satisfaction. It completes transactions and fills the world with action. It's attracted to the cunning but from the passive it stays running. Call it Jesus, it feeds the multitude and can save your world.

Often tried, vilified, chastised and despised but like the sun it always rises. So, in my hunt for more than my portion, I give my devotion to what is used to judge man, apart from his tan.

Understand my sentiments are dime a dozen amongst deprived brothers and malnourished cousins.

Meditation of the Damned   *Oneike Barnett*

I must confess, regurgitating this feeling from my chest, this thing for which I so yearn is valueless. Yet in our eyes it's so valuable, it conjures illusions that makes us comfortable and our bitter realities palatable; and our rigid lives, pliable and defiable. Substantial amounts make us unreliable.

Stumbled on a few, now I'm asking "who are you?" Not giving a fuck who is who, or mindful of the things I do, deluded.

Mask off, I shouldn't have changed like the change I got, which on the grand scale isn't a lot. But instead, pick sense from my dollar and be humble, not fumble or fall. Yea though I weigh the pros and the cons, I still want it all, millions.

Sheeples

Playing of instruments, the sweet sounds of Pianos, Guitars and Drums. Singing, dancing to a false sense of freedom. Captives so long not knowing what it's truly like to be free, following a path laid for us a subliminal journey.

Global positioning system trapped in our minds, living in this fantasy world, you can't see the signs. Adapting a new fad like geese going north, seasonal animals, delusionary smart.

Electromagnetic waves like radios they keep us in tuned, headed their direction without correction. We are all going down, too much demagoguery, mentally bound. Programmable organisms, walking dead, overwhelmed by technological madness, sadness, despair.

Fictional characters floating everywhere, burdened by debt and obligations, quicksand is our ground. Blindly dependent and imitative, slavish is the noun.

Sticking with the herd yet praying for release, keeping contempt in our thoughts, not wearing it on our fleece.

Stranded

You are far way out, no one can hear your loudest screams or shouts. Shipwrecked, cast away, with thoughts of being rescued any day now, but your biggest question is "How; what's a miracle?"

To a person who doesn't believe, hope is useless without faith, so you meditate. Harnessing the power that's within you, you are alive with work to do all it takes to survive.

Making it this far you stand a chance, the glint at the end of the tunnel, a life changing glance. Every step you take it's as if that glint takes ten, frustrated, fatigued from going around in circles again.

Diligently persevering, patience becomes your friend, your weapon, your tool, the entire mode in which you function.

Taking deep breaths, relaxing yourself, astonished at what you hear; no longer panicking or bewildered, displaying no fear.

Distorted look on your face from the unpalatable taste of abandonment and neglect, seeing every aspect of the empty shells around you. Realising its real, all the tension you feel, resisting the urge to squeal.

It's not a dream! So, you will never wake up, just have to smell the roses; oasis seems to be everywhere but imitation poses.

Your adrenaline hasn't kicked in yet, don't fret, you're going to make it. Staying tuned to your senses is all you need, last of a dying breed. With a rampant, rapacious appetite to succeed, so you will.

For every new day I'm thankful, with the essence of life my tank is full. No matter the weather I continue my quest, inhaling air in my lungs, knowing I'm blessed.

It's a blessing, a gift that I appreciate very much, utilizing my senses - hearing, seeing, smelling, tasting and touch. The supernatural life force flowing through my veins, keeps the cogs turning in my brain so I know I serve a purpose.

Don't own it, don't control it, though bestowed upon me. Being still, meditating, so with my third eye I see the true world and me, the embodiment of infinite possibilities, yes doing my best.

I have so much to live for, already lost all I had to lose, filled with bliss not blues, still retain the choice to choose. Content with mine, nothing lasts forever, that's fine. For every new day I'm thankful, with the essence of life my tank is full.

Displaying smiles as I traverse these miles, heart filled with benevolence, spreading love throughout my existence. Philanthropically motivated, selfish indulgence is overrated.

The sun rises in the east, wind blows from the west where the sun rests, awaken to a new day of chess. Alone? No, I don't exist on my own, heading for the stratosphere parts unknown; life speaks to me.

The Love of Hate

Love, are you not supposed to be good? Then why do you hurt so bad? Am I supposed to be this empty? Why am I even so sad? Hate, are you not supposed to be bad? Then why do you feel so good?

So satisfying, so gratifying, this may sound weird but I know I'm not lying. Love had me bound, scattering my emotions around, constant suffocation, I thought I would drown.

Ripping me apart, how did I get caught? Senseless affections destroyed my heart. Shock waves in my head, my eyes have turned red. From continuous crying, I feel like I'm dying. Love don't love me.

Hate loosed me, clear eyes now I see; resuscitation rescuing me, numbing my wounds. I'm ice cold, seizing control of tainted emotions from my afflicted soul.

My heart scabbed over and healed, now it's ten times as thick; I got rid of the infection, love made me sick.

Anaesthetics in my veins, now I'm pain-free, this is just my opinion, you don't have to agree. Hate don't hate me.

Behind the Eyelids

As I look to the hills from whence cometh my health, I thought to myself – "Is it worth bargaining for wealth, my well being?" That's priceless. In doing so am I not senseless? Should I not abandon my quest and settle for less, knowing its more? In retrospect, is there really a difference between the rich and the poor, besides delusions of grandeur?

My head aches; surrounded by fakes, my body shakes. Inflated egos, no need for spare yet I'm here. No rebirth, just a god on earth, spitting the truth for what it's worth. It is dirt cheap trying to wake the majority that are asleep, but they already gave their societal gods their souls to keep.

No joke, hated when you're woke, chastised when you believe the lies perceived by your eyes. Blasphemy is the cries. Cold world, having sexual relations with kids while posing with an old girl. These rulers are lascivious.

Poison is what they're giving us. If its not Ebola, Corona or Aids, its cancerous. Cantankerous beings willing to gain full control by any means necessary, so we're collected like tooth by the tooth fairy.

Hiding behind his dollar so he doesn't seem scary, but contrary to popular belief, his novocaine cause grief not relief. Taking something that doesn't belong to him makes him a 'what you may call it'. Oh shit! you died before you wake, so your soul you forfeit.

Cold Truth

My thoughts flow through my pen, my thoughtful pen writes stories of now and then. I tried to find love but what I was looking for either shape shifted, got stolen, or vanished into thin air.

Sentiments weighed me down like a lead-filled backpack on my back, while climbing the Mount Everest of life's deadly terrain. Without it I acclimatized to the elevation with ease, ice can't freeze; love can't survive below zero degrees, it needs warmth.

How far you are, how far pings the signal on my radar? As I leave sentiments behind, control of self inclined; mastermind with a master's mind, I mastered my talents, intrepid, logically selected, rationally directed.

The path to a peaceful and sociable existence is self interest, so I appeal to their ideals, reciprocity is the key to the vault of retribution, therefore your contribution to safekeeping will be valuable to you, invest wisely.

My interest now lies in acquiring paper, not just for writing, but frugal spending. Currency is trending, so banks I'm befriending.

Surrounded by earners my earnings go around in a circle, monetary momentum, residual income is the outcome. Friend for cash, so I went and got some. Addicted, I want more. Being poor isn't for me, nothing is free.

Implying the top is cold and lonely, you've never been there. Wealthy people are here, my new peers for a new me. As for my old peers and old me, old is the operative word, I outgrew them.

Just short of too late, I made it; just short of too great, trying to be the greatest, nothing but A+. If you grade this, let me say this - if lack of money is the root of all evil, I'm good.

Fluidity

Dying leaves are frightened by Autumn wind. I'm Autumn wind. Like trees in Autumn, I shed my leaves, disconnecting myself from energy thieves.

Reconnecting with my source, flourishing after my divorce, everyone wants to know my florist. It's Spring time to bloom, plus holding on equals my doom, so letting go comes naturally. New leaves grow, better energy flow, from death comes life.

My Caterpillar morphed into a butterfly and flew away from moral decay; with the rising sun is a new day. Then the twilight becomes night and the moon shines bright, then all is revealed that was hidden in the daylight.

With a sense of peace my rough seas became calm and navigable, my inhabitable heart became warm and habitable. All that was insipid became palatable and digested. I profited from the time I invested in emotional and social intelligence, hence managing my survival portfolio, diversifying without trying.

My revival is sublime, lofty are my thoughts, mastering the arts of patience and timing. My climbing is impeccable, on the edge taking chances with mathematical advances. My skills improve as I execute calculated moves.

To the summit, to the zenith, I'll submit like never before. It's like a NASA rocket is embedded in my core, which explains my perennial need to soar.

Meditation of the Damned, I was dammed up but my strength grew, I broke through and kept running.

Ghetto Mentality

If we keep fighting over this plot instead of planting the little we've got, it will eventually be our burial plot, like Dove Cot. Drenched in blood, perpetuating the death cycle of wanting to be don's and soldiers to battle ourselves, decimate ourselves, though destitute.

My childhood friend is now my enemy because he lives on the opposite side of the fence. Hence, he must die; but why? Is that reason enough? Aren't we squatters occupying captured space? The disgrace and disgust, is us; opposite sides of the same coin.

The 'don't' should be you and me not letting ourselves be led by the blind. Only darkness we'll find, open your mind. Being born in these slums don't make us bums. If you don't work, how will you eat? Stop twiddling your thumbs!

We have guns and ammunition galore, still starving and poor, yet our ambition is to acquire more; to destroy the already dying, to bring more anguish to those already crying.

Magnifying the heat on ourselves, even though we're already frying.

We can make a positive change. It's time we have ample, each of us could be a sample example of what our future ghettos should be - a plethora of educated parents and children living together in unity. Striving to better themselves and community. Spreading love, joy, peace and happiness, relinquishing hate, jealousy and envy.

Remember nothing is impossible under the sun, and we will be held accountable when it's all over and done.

Humility Rules

I wasn't this self-absorbed, but now I'm feeling myself. Gaining wealth with failing health, I caress myself feeling ways I've never felt.

I wasn't this self-absorbed, its unusual. Checking my surroundings, the feeling isn't mutual. To my peers, my actions have changed my attitude. Rearranged, now I'm condescending and cocky, thinking everyone's sloppy, no one's happy.

Went from crammed buses to first class flights, pillow top mattress, fuck sleepless nights. Soaring to new heights, blurred sights.

I wasn't this self-absorbed, but now silver is behind transparency, so I'm all I see. Looking in this mirror on the wall, pride comes before the fall. Could have given help to all who ask and didn't ask but I refused.

Propelled by greed, kept what I didn't need, left starving mouths hungry. Thinking you should level up with a empty cup, separate level of eyes, so you're categorized. Bottom feeders what's up?

Or should I say - "what's down?". After removing meat, not even bone touches the ground. No sketches were dropped when I'm on top.

Thumping my chest, wearing designers, jewelry and cars super expensive, nothing less until life puts me to the test, now my actions I second guess, falling off.

I am this self-absorbed, this is the true me, money allowed everyone to see right through me. Before, people use to say "your selfish", I was like – "who me?" Then I realized this is who I be, it's not a new me.

Karma exposed me with drama, have me wishing I was much calmer, timber like Osama. Now there is no one to lend a helping hand, only to help me down.

Mocked, jeered, followed by loud laughter; "look at the clown, put him six feet underground". Death is the noun that causes my heart to pound, abnormally.

This is what they all wished for me, struck with utter blight, I'm contrite; with an abundance of food for my thoughts. Can I enjoy the meal?

#
Lascivious

———•·•◆•·•———

I hadn't had wine in a minute, so I drank a bottle in under a minute. There she was, she's beautiful with supple breast, thick thighs, brown eyes and a sexy camel toe, just so you know. I just want to go from where babies flow.

"Please sweetie, let me hit it" I found myself saying out loud; so loud it echoes. I want it! I want it! I want it!

Oh shit! She aroused the beast in me, pointing straight ahead is mini me. Eager to reach his destination like a train at the station, waiting to penetrate her dark moist tunnel.

My voice crisp, as in her ear I whisper. My confidence grew as I kiss her and assist her out of her cloths, then whisk her to the place where magic glows, I suppose.

Foreplay was the first order of the day, on her nipples my tongue played, her heart racing as if afraid.

I reassured her I'm like the Bank of Nova Scotia, she is safe with me, she showed her safe to me. Realizing I have the key, I gently opened just to see and be amongst her treasures, not ruffling her feathers.

I proceeded to explore her inner secrets that Victoria hid. So happy like a kid in a candy store, she said "more", the command I adore. So, I took more and more.

Every piece made me wiser, as pressures mounted like a geyser. She quaked, causing a tsunami. Like Mount Vesuvius uninterrupted, I erupted, shooting spawns of cupid, winning the bid for her heart's security.

Way Up

Way up, staying high as if you're flying, eyes blood shot as if you were crying. O.G. Kush barbiturates in your brain to sustain, deviating from thoughts of saving the world. How can you, when you break bread with people who have a reptilian indifference for human lives?

Life is life, long am I wrong for not wanting to play their apathetic games. Sitting across from the devil himself, promising wealth for your health, a pot of gold for your soul.

Leprechaun, magical like a Unicorn. Four leaf clover, gifted if you chose; you'll have wrist and neck froze, rock the latest designer cloths. Flooded with superficial charms and beautiful women on your arms.

Aiming for the fame. Who can you blame for receiving less than you gave? No profit, blindly dependent, imitative. Feeling like a foreigner, though a native in your own skin. Drinking gin like its holy water, shouting "Our Father who art in heaven". Sin up to your neck, cause and effect. Is the sacrifice worth the check?

Way up, gliding, hiding from yourself, too weak to go seek the truth right before your eyes, disguised amongst lies. No needle in a hay stack, the façade is to go hard and waste eight stacks, while they invest their stacks.

Airheads, they know this, we're livestock, you noticed. Consuming their fabrications, subjects of mass manipulation, brainwashed clean of knowledge. Impaired food for the Arachnids, trapped on their web, waiting to be devoured with natural instincts. Overpowered, you're slowly digested.

Pretense

They said I'm dead, it reverberates in my head. They said I'm dead, my heart deteriorated, my mind is worse, contentment eludes me. Is this a blessing or a curse? I can't eat, though I know this is deceit, not defeat. Feeling emasculated, out of balance, off beat.

Hanged by betrayal, trust tied the noose. Love was my captor, forgiveness tried to cut me loose, mercy tried to declare a truce, but they wasn't so lucky. In the electric chair they fried, regret couldn't hide, she succumbed to suicide; we all died.

Numb, I can't feel what I am. It's a rotten wound that won't heal, with suffering as deep and hollow as an empty well, an empty shell. Am I in hell? I can't tell. What must I do to get well?

It's as if I'm going under; but am I really above? Transcendent, looking down on my afflictions like science fiction, revenge is my addiction. I need rehab, I need to live again. I need a defused ear and a defused brain; no doubt the sun will shine again, but this isn't rain. It's rain, it's liquid sun.

What's the victory of the race without the run, the effort, the struggle? To persevere, I am here. My moral compass wasn't working, so I updated, mutated, saved me for me, cause without me there can be no I. Without tears I can't cry, so I ripped the glands from my eyes, unloaded my burdens, said my goodbyes to the past that past.

The things I tossed, the things I lost and repercussions that cost me my time. Don't worry I'm fine, claiming what's mine, what belongs to me. What goes around comes around, what goes up, must come down; these are songs to me.

He who laughs last, laughs best. I aced this test, chewed, swallowed and digest, while they regressed. No wonder they're mad. Lazarus in their midst, no wonder they're sad. They wished me bad, while pretending they were the best friends I ever had.

Now I know better, never depended on any of them. I'm a go getter, trend setter, still setting trends. World please be aware of back-stabbing love ones and friends, they're abundant.

Pandemic

Mass murders in the disguise of a pandemic, the world leaders are indeed sick. Magicians, this is a fatal trick from the great mathematicians. They remove the veil from our eyes, yet left it over our noses. You can see death, but never smell when it decomposes.

Radios, televisions, spreading fear in the air, there's no cure says propaganda, to our despair. Stay away from everyone, stay indoors, practice social distancing. The most important life you can save is yours; but what about the doctors? Who's going to save them from this cataclysmic event, this man-made phlegm?

Corona is her name, but man is the true virus. In retrospect of history there is nothing as deadly as us. Millions must die, all in the name of profit. They're more than seven billion people and to sustain us, they say the world is unfit. So, reduce it they must, amidst sobs and cries; Covid-19 is a natural cause, if you believe the lies.

The whole world is on lock down, their plan in full effect. A vaccine is coming to save us from prior neglect, to receive just genuflect, to reduce the adverse effects on humanity.

America thought it was over the hump, until it bumped into Trump, who entered China - the synthetic vagina, implanted this weapon in mother Earth's womb as he was told, sealing our doom.

The deception messed with our perception. Fingerprint, there won't be one with gloves on. Mask on your face and dead witnesses, it's a cold case. Let's take this time to embrace our love ones and neglected peers, whom we haven't seen for years.

Call them and in your lives re-install them. Go beyond and above to spread love, its very necessary. All you think was a necessity, you're now coping without, that's scary. Contrary to popular belief, the adverse effects of vanity is brief, love is everlasting.

In spite of our forced mobile fasting, diverse life in the greater world continues unaffected. Animals and insects still go where they want to go, the wind still blows, look at the flourishing flora and fauna it shows, the sun still glows. The swash and back wash of the ocean is still in motion. Then how important is man? Let it sink in, for the evilest of evils, good will always win.

REACH OUT TO THE AUTHOR
*with your feedback, queries, orders and requests for signing
& bookings*

barnettsfarm357@gmail.com

Made in the USA
Columbia, SC
18 August 2021